Unleash

CASH FLOW MOJO

The Business Owner's Guide to Predicting, Planning, and Controlling Your Company's Cash Flow

Sandra S. Simmons

Published in the USA by
Money Management Solutions, Inc.
4001 Santa Barbara Blvd., #358
Naples, FL 34104

ISBN 978-0-9770771-9-9

Praise For *Unleash Your Cash Flow Mojo*

I've been a CPA since 1984 and have always used "old school" methods to analyze cash flow. By that, I mean managing cash and other assets based upon historical accounting statements. I've been a colleague of Sandra's for four years and she really opened my eyes as to how to best manage a firm's cash resources in an optimal manner. Sandra is a true pioneer in the field of cash flow and wealth management.

Kent Harlan, CPA – Ozarks Capital Funding, Inc., Springfield, MO

****

This method works. It worked for my company several years ago, I personally know the owners of other companies Sandra has turned around with it, and it will work for any company, or personal budget, for that matter.

The key is the sub-title: The Business Owner's Guide to Predicting, Planning and Controlling Your Company's Cash Flow. Most business owners work in reverse – using accounting to look at where the money went (often, more than what came in…), rather than PLANNING and CONTROLLING.

Sandra knows her stuff. If you want to be wealthy, you need to implement the process of Cash Flow Mojo.

Rosalie Hamilton, Founder & President of Expert Communications, Inc. and author of *The Expert Witness Marketing Book.*

****

I have used this software program "Cash Flow Mojo" for a Fortune 100 company that does a gross of 2.5M a year. It enabled me to turn the company around and move it from red to black within one year. I was also able to establish a reserve account of over $75,000.

If you follow the Cash Flow Mojo program, you will definitely be able to work yourself out of debt, set-up various reserve and savings accounts and increase your profitability.

The program itself is very user friendly and easy to use.

I personally have known Sandra Simmons for several years and she knows what she is talking about. Her expertise in this area is beyond compare and I have personally witnessed what she has been able to do for various companies.

Kathleen Lettau, President, Perfect Accounting Service, Inc. Naples, FL

Dedication

This book is dedicated to

my family, my friends, and

my husband, Brian Dawson

who understands my passion

for this subject and encouraged me.

Introduction

Welcome to the age of business cash flow management in the new economy. For decades, business owners have been using century-old accounting and forecasting tools to try to manage their financial affairs. Yet these old tools have done little to help them peer into the future and have offered few guideposts with which to predict which way the winds of finance would blow for their companies.

Some time ago I realized that, without guideposts and tools to predict, plan and control the financial future of their companies, businesses owners were very likely to get into trouble, or fail financially, despite how well their business was doing at any given time

How is it that some businesses manage to flourish and become financially successful, and yet many do not? How do they accomplish what seems to be magical success?

It is a matter of viewing cash flow management with a bit of a different viewpoint, learning that the old tools, while useful for certain things, are not adequate by themselves, and not making the fatal mistakes that many business owners make in managing their company's money.

What are the qualities that empower a business owner to manage cash flow so that they flourish financially? They are simple yet powerful actions that unleash the mojo (magical powers) of substantial, sustainable cash flow.

In this book you will discover that unleashing the cash flow mojo is within the grasp of every business owner who cares to make use of it. Because you are reading this book, you have a better chance than others of unleashing the mojo and using it to good effect.

Why I wrote this book:

1. You need to know this stuff to survive and flourish financially in your business.

2. Business, especially small business, is the backbone of any economy. If small business fails, we all fail. I don't want you to fail. The country needs you solvent and viable.

This book is not a motivational tool. It is a guide to a new way of thinking about and handling money. It contains the steps of a system and explains how to avoid the fatal mistakes inherent in managing the cash flow in a business. It even goes so far as to guide you through reversing mistakes you have made with money in the past.

There are tools introduced in this book to help you apply the system, unleash your mojo, and accomplish the steps outlined in this guide in a minimal amount of time. Some are free and some carry a price. It is up to you to decide whether or not you will use the tools.

Just a note here: I sometimes interchange the phrase "cash flow management" with "money management." In this system they mean exactly the same thing.

Of all the questions business owners ask me, the most common question I get is "How can I make more money AND increase my profits?"

Most business owners think that increasing sales is the answer, and while that certainly is part of the equation, it's not the WHOLE answer. A business can bring in lots of income and still be struggling to survive.

On the other hand, some businesses bring in a comparatively modest amount of income and are in *great* financial shape.

Why is this?

It's simple. It has everything to do with how the business USES the income that determines its financial condition.

If you're like most business owners, you are super busy running your company.

So let me ask you a question. How much time do you spend planning how to utilize the most important resource your business has — its cash flow — to guarantee you achieve your financial goals?

Cash flow management *planning* **is the missing step.** It's the step that business owners were never trained to do. That's why I wrote this book.

My intention is very simple. After reading this book, I expect you to implement the behavioral and procedural changes it covers so that you gain complete control of your company's financial future. When you do that you can make your business resistant to any negative economic situations that rage around it now or in the future

We dare not allow economic conditions to break the back of small business. While you cannot control the economy in general, you CAN control the economy of your business by understanding and practicing correct cash flow management. Harnessing and using what you learn from this book will give you **Cash Flow Mojo.**

Contents

What is Cash Flow Mojo?

The definition of the word mojo is **magical powers**.

When you have cash flow mojo you have an understanding of, and are applying, all of the concepts and procedures of correct cash flow management to your company's best financial advantage. The areas of application include:

- Budgeting.
  This is not the type of budgeting that only means belt tightening or denying yourself anything fun.

- Setting the correct income planning target *to do better than break-even.*
  The majority of business owners get this one wrong from the start.

- Doing sales planning and promotional planning to drive sales upward.
  There is a science to this that is simple yet often neglected

- Cutting discretionary expenses to free up cash flow.
  Hint: promotion and marketing are NOT discretionary. They are mandatory.

- Getting out of debt or avoiding getting into debt.
  This one is a piece of cake when you have the cash flow mojo juiced up on the finance line.

- Avoiding common mistakes that can be financially fatal and reversing those types of mistakes you made in the past.
Every business owner has made a few mistakes. But what you learn from making the mistakes and what you do in the future will determine your company's ability to not only survive, but thrive.

- Saving money in what my clients and I fondly call "buckets of cash" designated for specific things.
This is the fun part where you can actually start sleeping better at night just knowing that you have the cash flow mojo going on and that you are going to be better than just "okay."

- Thinking and planning in the present and in futures. This directly relates to those buckets of cash you are going to start filling up in your company.

- Not wasting a dime or spending money needlessly. This one is a biggie for those of you who make enough money that you think you can afford to waste some, or even give it away before you have met your personal goals.

- Setting financial goals for the future, and keeping the discipline in week after week so you can and do reach those goals, and then setting new ones.

This one is totally under your control from the get-go, but may be the hardest one to put in and keep in.

When you have all that in place, and are thinking with, and operating with, the correct management of cash flow, then you *will* have cash flow mojo going on. Doing all of these things correctly is simpler than you can possibly imagine and more powerful than you can believe...until you've done it. Applying what you learn from this book will help you do it.

Adopting a Different Operating Basis

Your most basic viewpoint shift requires your knowing and understanding the difference between **Accounting Versus Cash Flow Management Planning**

For many, the subject of accounting seems complicated and mysterious. In fact, accounting is simply recording what occurred with the money in a company or a household. It answers the questions of how much money came in and where that money was spent.

Any standard accounting system and the reports it generates is actually a look back in the past. The money came in, went out and is recorded after the fact. It tells you how much was made or lost, and how much is currently owed.

While this is important to know; and, because you have to report it to the taxing authorities, it can put the company or individual in a position of being controlled by the money, always making financial decisions based only on how much money is left in the bank and how much tax is going to be levied on the profit.

Being held hostage by your bank account balance is just not fun. Having to ask yourself, or your bookkeeper, "How much money do I have in the bank? Can I pay this bill?" is you being controlled by the money your accounting system says is available right now.

Cash flow management planning, on the other hand, is done by looking at today and toward the future. Planning occurs BEFORE the money comes in and BEFORE it is spent. This puts the company or individual in control of the money. And that is how it should be.

For any company, planning and implementing actions to make more income are essential.

Cost of living increases, rising prices and taxes eat away at modest income growth. Reducing expenses without reducing the ability to produce income is necessary to have a profitable company today. Using existing cash and resources in a way that prevents waste and generates more income is vital.

All of these actions require planning BEFORE doing. This is operating in the future.

Where did all the money go? Your accounting system tells you that.

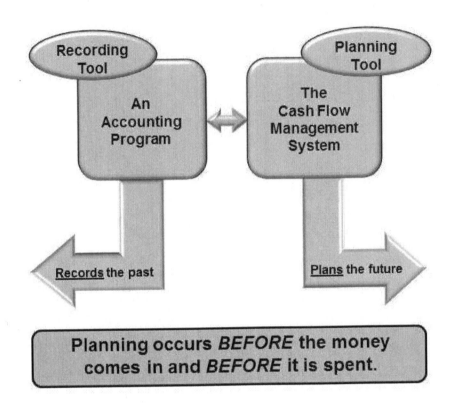

Planning occurs *BEFORE* the money comes in and *BEFORE* it is spent.

Cash Flow Mojo® Tip #1

Stop making financial decisions based only on how much money you have in your bank account.

How much money will be coming in? How can it best be used to increase the long term survival potential of a company and its individual employees?

The answers to these questions require frequent, consistent, and careful cash flow planning and management. By consistently applying the principles in this book, you can quickly develop the skills to do the correct cash flow management actions for your company.

Testimonial

"Less than 3 months ago the likelihood of paying off a huge debt without borrowing money seemed impossible, much less figuring out how to continue running our business without any money. Our production statistics were down, the quality of our work was poor, jobs were not profitable, acquiring new jobs was at a stand-still and we were BLOCKED.

Using this Cash Flow Management Software, we did our weekly planning faithfully. It brought us understanding of what caused our financial difficulties in the first place, peace of mind through a very stressful period, and the ability to get through each week with a plan of action that allowed us to systematically work ourselves into a better condition in just 3 short months. Now the contracts are flowing in, we have qualified personnel, great profitable work, haven't had to borrow a penny to pay off debts and now have a very simple and workable software system to flourish and prosper." - P. A.

Flourish (verb intransitive) to do well and be prosperous; to be in a state of activity and production; to reach a height of development or influence; to increase in health, wealth, happiness, honor, comfort or whatever is desirable - Webster Third International Dictionary © 1909

The Most Important Question You Need to Answer

Typically a business owner will reconcile the bank account in their accounting system in order to find out how much money is in the bank account, and then pay the bills based on pressures being put on the business. In any given week the pressure can be extreme to cover payroll, the rent or mortgage, a credit card payment that's due, and a vendor who is screaming for money and threatening to cut off deliveries of supplies you need to produce more income.

Little thought is given to what next week's needs are going to be in the face of current extreme financial pressures.

So how should you be managing your cash flow to not only pay this week's demands, but to also plan for next week's and next month's demands *and* start filling up those buckets of cash I mentioned earlier?

The correct cash flow management cycle begins with knowing your real income planning target. This is discovered by building a budget, and making sure that the budget includes everything needed for the company to operate and to become financially secure.

When a new client hires me to do one-on-one cash flow management coaching, one of the first questions I typically ask is, **"How much cash do you need to bring in to run your operation each week?"** I usually get a period of silence, and then they get a pad and pencil and noodle around some figures. Finally they will spit out a number and I write that down. Then we do the drill to find out what their cash flow actually needs to be for their business to do better than break even.

When we compare the two numbers they are often radically different. I have found over the past 20+ years that the business owner typically UNDER estimates what they need to bring in by 13 to 25% depending on the type of business they are in.

If they are operating on a target that is too low, then they are PLANNING TO GO BROKE.

The income planning target needs to be a weekly target. This not only helps you run much tighter control on the money; it also gives you a smaller number, where a larger number may tend to make you freeze up and decide something deadly like, "I can never make that target."

Cash Flow Mojo® Tip #2

Know exactly how much income you really need to bring in each week to do much better than break even.

There can be a huge difference in your, your managers', and your employees' reaction to being told that they have to produce $35,000 in sales this week, versus being told they have to produce $151,666 in sales this month. A smaller target is just flat out easier to confront.

The method you use to figure out what that weekly target needs to be is simple, and thought provoking and can lead you to some realizations about your business that should have been smacking you in the head a long time ago. Let's go over what goes on the list of items that add up to the correct income planning target to do better than break even.

1. Cost of Goods Sold
Items that appear on your P&L (raw materials, specialty supplies, etc.)

2. Overhead Expenses
These appear on your P&L (HINT: make a separate line item for the business owner's salary separate from a line item for the employees' payroll)

3. Long term Liability Debts

These appear on your Balance Sheet (mortgage, equipment financed, etc.)

4. Revolving Credit Card Debt and Lines of Credit

These appear on your Balance Sheet

5. A line item for an increase in the Cost of Doing Business

(Costs increase 8 – 12% a year, so I recommend that you make this weekly figure 8% of your gross income in the past year.)

6. A line item for Emergency Savings

(This is your 1st Bucket of Cash - I recommend that you make this weekly figure 1% of your average weekly gross income in the past 12 months)

7. A line Item For Business Expansion Savings

(This is your 2nd Bucket of Cash - I recommend that you make this weekly figure 5% of your average weekly gross income in the past 12 months)

8. A line Item For Legal Defense and Taxes Savings

(This is your 3rd Bucket of Cash - I recommend that you make this weekly figure 5% of your average weekly gross income in the past 12 months)

9. A line Item For Savings (Reserves)

(This is your 4th Bucket of Cash - I recommend that you make this weekly figure 5% of your average weekly gross income in the past 12 months)

Add up all these items and do the math on how much that totals on a weekly basis and you'll know for sure what your Income Target needs to be to do much better than break even.

Recalculate this list based on updated figures every three to four months to account for changes in your business so you'll always have the correct target number.

Nobody goes into business just to pay bills and make their suppliers wealthy. You should PLAN to make a very nice profit. So the most important question you have to answer is **how much should your weekly income planning target be.**

Proven Truth

It's not *only* how much money you make. It's what you do with it that determines your financial condition.

Budgeting

Expense Calculation

Type of Expense	Annual
Emergency Account (1% Recommended)	522.22
Expansion Account (5% Recommended)	2,611.00
Legal & Tax Account (5% Recommended)	2,611.00
Savings Account (5% Recommended)	2,611.00
COGS – Cost of Goods Inventory	9,295.51
COGS – Cost of Goods Sold Labor	7,312.35
COGS – Cost of Goods Sold Supplies	3,893.89
Auto Expenses	5,915.12
Bank Service Charges	179.00
Computer Peripherals	135.89

When You Are Freaked Out by Your Income Target

The first thing you should do is divide the last 12 months of gross income your company made by 52 weeks to see how close to or far away from your Income Target your actual income truly is. This can be a huge shock to a lot of business owners. It really freaks them out.

The good news is that knowing the real target puts you in positive control and only then can you go about doing the actions to move the income up to where it needs to be to make the target.

That can be facilitated by going over the financials and discovering where costs can be cut that will not have a negative impact on the company's ability to make income.

I often take on a new business owner client and discover that they never even look at the financial statements produced by their accounting system. I find that this is because they don't know how to read the financials and determine what they mean, so I spend time on that in my coaching. I can review a P&L and Balance sheet and in about 20 minutes of conversation with the business owner, I can tell what is wrong and what needs to be done to repair the finances of the company.

Often the repair involves cutting back on expenses in a way that it does not harm production, stashing extra cash for income building activities and covering future financial emergencies.

A colleague of mine defines a financial emergency as a predictable expense that was never planned for.

Financial Emergency (Definition)

A predictable expense that was never planned for.

You know that the building is going to need a new roof or a new air conditioning system some day in the future. You know that your delivery van is going to have to be replaced at the 250,000 mile mark. You know that some equipment is going to break down at some point. Yet no cash is saved up to cover that expected future expense, so when the roof starts leaking or the equipment fails the predictable expense has the appearance of a sudden emergency.

Cash Flow Mojo® Tip #3

Don't cut expenses in places that harms production and sales.

The negative differential (gap between the weekly income and the weekly expenses) can also be handled by raising prices, adding profitable products or services that are in high demand, and having a weekly sales and income planning meeting with your staff to plan exactly how to hit the income planning target for the week. Read on to find out what to cover in your sales and income planning meetings.

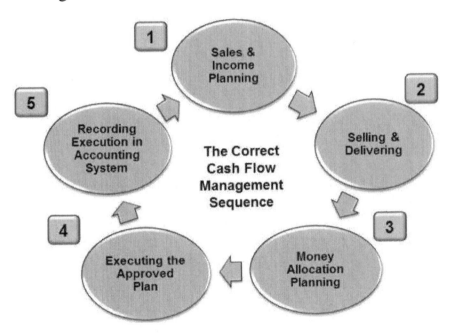

Sales and Income Planning

Armed with your correct Income Target, the first step of the cash flow mojo management cycle is done at the beginning of each and every business week. It is called the Sales and Income Planning Meeting.

It is composed of four parts:

1. Evaluate the results of last week's sales and income planning session. Did the sales teams hit their targets? Did collections meet their quota? Did the promotion deliver the expected results? If not, why not? Only when you figure that out can you correct things and keep the sales moving up.

2. Assign your sales personnel their weekly sales targets / quotas based on your income target. Get each person who is selling to figure out and write out a plan of how they are going to bring their assigned $ target of sales into the company. This can be supported by your actions in step 4 below.

3. If you have receivables to collect, give your collections staff their targets of how much receivables they need to collect this week. Have them work out who they will collect from and how much in order to make their targets.

4. Decide what you are going to promote and how you are going to promote it to bring sales into the company. Will you promote a new item, promote a popular item to upsell an add-on, or offer a special deal on some inventory you need to get rid of by bundling it with a very popular item? What media vehicles will you use to promote and how much will that cost? How big of a return can you reasonably expect to get from that promotion using that media type?

Let your sales people know what and how you are promoting so they can use that to help them sell. Later we'll talk about how to fund marketing during the rest of the planning cycle.

Have you ever cut back or cut off the marketing funding in your company in an effort to save money? If you have, then let me ask you this: If you aren't talking to your current and prospective customers through marketing, and your competitors are talking to them, who are they more likely to buy from?

Of course you should make sure that whatever you are promoting will bring in adequate profits, and that the media type chosen to advertise will pull in enough sales to way more than pay for the costs. But marketing is not a discretionary expense. It's mandatory.

You can't sit there and wait for the phone to ring or for a customer to walk through the door without telling them repeatedly that your company is there and that you have what they are ready, willing and able to buy.

Customers these days are not only smart, they are fickle. They'll buy from the person who is talking to them through marketing even if their friends referred them to you. The first thing they will do is go online to see if you have a website. If you don't, they will think you may not be a legitimate business, or that you may be too small a business to handle their needs.

Sales and Income Planning

Sales Target

Weekly Income Pl

Product / Location Description	Sales Person(s)	Quantity

Total Expected Sales Inc

[Add New Sales Item] [Save Changes]

Collections Target

Account Name or ID Number	Total Amount Owed	Amt. Expected to Collect
	0.00	0.00

Total Expected Collections Income This Week: 0.00
Sum of Expected Sales and Collections This Week: 0.00
Over / Under Weekly Income Planning Target: 0.00

[Add New Collections Item] [Save Changes]

Advertising and Promotion Planning

Product / Offer Description	Retail Price	Prod. & Labor Cost	Co
	0.00	0.00	

Expected Unit Sales	Expected Profit	Media Type	Med
0	0.00		

Total Expected Net Profit from Advertising and

Post-it® Notes and Promo

I've seen business owners who go on a rampage about not buying Post-it notes because they are expensive and they have the staff put lots of time and attention on cutting up used paper to make scrap paper to substitute for post-it notes, just to save a few bucks.

I don't know about you, but to me paying someone well over minimum wage to spend time cutting up scrap paper to use as Post-it notes can end up costing more than the Post-it notes themselves. Then this same business owner will cut back or cut off spending on marketing which is his best chance to reach customers and make more sales so that he *can* afford the Post-it notes if he wants them.

Cash Flow Mojo® Tip #4

Do your sales and income planning at the
beginning of every business week.

Sales and Delivery

Once the income planning is done for the week, you should NOT spend the rest of the week thinking about or worrying about money. Customers are very perceptive. They can tell when your attention is on them, concerned about satisfying their needs, or if you are seeing them just as a wallet full of cash.

They are fickle too. They will go where they feel like they can get better service and are treated like their needs are the most important consideration.

So after the sales and income planning is done at the beginning of the business week, step 2 of the correct cash flow management cycle (see Illustration on page 16) is to spend the week selling your products and services to your customers and delivering excellent customer service that keeps them coming back for more and referring your business to others.

So, no worrying about the money during the week! Worrying doesn't make sales. Worrying about money never made a dime of income for anyone, plus it's stressful.

Treating your customers right, and offering them what they need, makes sales.

Plus your staff is tuned into your mood. And if you are worried about the money, they'll be worried about it too, and that can make a bad situation even worse.

Proven Truth

Customers are repelled by desperation, and attracted to confidence and certainty.

How to Use Your Cash Flow to Achieve YOUR Financial Goals

Okay, at the end of the business week, we move on to the formula for the next step; allocation planning. This occurs once the week's income has been received and has cleared the bank.

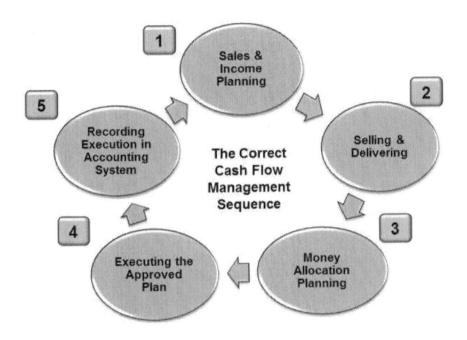

Allocate means to portion out, assign, or earmark. The formula for allocating your money to your best financial advantage is a process that follows an exact sequence of steps so you can achieve your financial goals. This is an area where smart money managers, like millionaires and their financial staff, excel.

Cash Flow Mojo® Tip #5

Take an active role in the weekly cash flow management decisions.

It requires having a plan, following the plan, and having the discipline to stick with the plan no matter what. That takes courage and commitment, and the ability to say NO when something, or someone, tries to pull you off the plan.

I want to go over the basic formula in sequence so you'll fully get this. It's very simple and very powerful and is the heart of correct cash flow management.

The following illustration is an abbreviated snapshot of how the software system's cash flow controller helps you allocate your cash flow to your advantage.

You can refer to this illustration as we go through this sequence with an invented company.

$32,000		Gross Income This Week
-	12	Bank Charges
-	3,200	Sales Commissions
-	1,078	Credit Card Merchant Fees
$27,710		Adjusted Gross Income (AGI)
-	8,464	Payroll & Payroll Taxes This Week
-	2,320	Promotion Allocation This Week
-	4,434	16% Cash Savings for Future
-	5,542	20% to Past Due Bills and Credit Debt
-	6,650	Allocation for Current and Future bills
$300		Balance Remaining of the AGI

You can see at the top of this illustration that the Gross Income for the week was $32,000. The first thing you have to remember when your company receives income is that not all the money comes in as yours to spend. If you look behind you there is a line of vendors with their hands out waiting for the share you promised to pay them.

Other examples: Once a month your bank might swipe some bank charges right out of your account. A customer is going to ask for a refund based on your guarantee. The credit card companies are going to sweep your account for the merchant fees you owe for the privilege of accepting credit cards, and your commission sales person who sold a job is going to want their commission.

You can see at the top of this illustration that the Gross Income for the week was "adjusted" by these payments, and the Adjusted Gross Income (AGI), which is the business owner's cash to spend for the week, is now $27,710.

The rest of the sequence is very simple, and very powerful. You can refer to the illustration while we cover the rest of the steps of the basic formula in sequence.

Payroll

The first item that gets allocated for out of the Adjusted Gross Income (AGI) is payroll, including the company's share of the payroll taxes. This figure includes the business owner's salary or draws. (Tip - If you pay payroll every other week, then on the weeks in between, try to set aside half of the anticipated payroll expense. This keeps you from scrambling for the funds to pay the full nut on the week payroll is due to be paid.)

Promotion

The next most important item is funding your marketing plan. (Tip - Figure out what it would cost to fund your ideal marketing plan to promote the way you know you should be promoting. Then divide that to get the weekly cost and carve out that amount each week to fund the plan.)

Pay Yourself First - Savings

Next is carving out the savings for the future. Ever hear the old adage "Pay yourself first?" Of course you have. Well, if you don't pay you into these funds, who will?

Remember we talked about the **Emergency Fund** to pay for predictable expenses that were never planned for? Here is where to do that. Set a goal of how much total you need that fund to be and what it will be used for (roof repair, new tires, A/C repairs, etc.) and try to set aside 1% of the AGI each week until that bucket of cash is up to the level you want. Then stop carving out for the emergency fund until you have to spend some of it to cover an "emergency" and then start again setting aside the 1% to replenish the "Emergency" bucket of cash.

Next is the **Expansion Account**. The recommendation is 5% of the AGI into this bucket of cash to grow the business and invest in things that ultimately produce more income:

- new equipment to increase production of a current product or service, or to add a new product or service,

- a down payment on a business building for your business if you are renting, or to open a second location;

- buying a building to lease to someone else if you already own your building, anything that will keep the business growing and the income going up.

Next is 5% into the **Legal and Tax Account**. This bucket of cash is for two purposes. Half is for self-insurance or paying for legal help that may be needed to keep the company safe. The other half is to pay taxes for the company.

Next, the **Reserves** of 5% into a savings account that is an additional safety net for the company that you try like the devil not to spend so it can be used as a long-term wealth building account. The funds in this account should be used to invest to make more money while keeping the principal safe from depletion.

Cash Flow Mojo® Tip #6

Don't work just to pay the bills. Have a long-term financial plan for the future.

And finally we allocate for paying credit debts and the bills.

Credit Debt

It is recommended to use 10 – 15% of the AGI to pay off revolving credit card debt. One of the most important things you can do to help a company survive is to stay out of the pay-for-life credit debt trap.

There is a difference between bad credit and good credit. Bad credit is using credit to buy something that gets used up or decreases in value. Good credit buys an asset that increases in value. An example of good debt is borrowing money short term to make the down payment on a building that will increase in value and possibly generate more income in lease fees.

I'm not saying don't use credit cards. I'm saying if you plan to use them, get into a position to pay off the full balance due when the statement arrives so you never pay interest on the purchases.

The best way to pay off credit card debt is to pay off the highest interest rate card first and then attack the next one until they are all paid off. Then be very careful to not put purchases on the cards that you have not set money aside to pay for when the statement arrives.

Past Due Bills

Next it is recommended to use 10 – 15% of the AGI to pay off past due bills. It's no fun to be behind the 8-ball using this week's income to pay last week's or last month's bills. It's very stressful, too. So to get on top of, and then in front of the 8-ball, use 10 – 15% of the weekly AGI to pay off those past due bills as fast as possible, while also keeping up with the allocation for current bills.

Current Bills

From the remaining balance of the week's income, you need to use a portion to pay current bills. The most important current bills are the ones that keep the lights on and the doors open – like utilities – and licenses and insurances that allow you to operate in safety – malpractice insurance, medical board licenses, etc.

Proven Truth

Managed money works harder, goes further,
and accomplishes more than money that is
spent without a plan.

The Cardinal RULE

The most important rule of this cash flow management game is that you cannot spend more money than you brought in and that cleared the bank during the week. This means that if you used the company debit card to buy lunch or a tank of gas, then you have to deduct that in the **Emergency Expenditures Paid** at the top of the cash flow controller window in the software, unless you put an expense account allowance for such things in the Bills and allocate to pay that bill every week.

Either way, those little expenditures like a tank of gas, lunch with a colleague or an emergency trip to the office supply store for a toner cartridge can add up to a couple of hundred dollars really fast, and once that money is spent, you can't spend it again.

If that means that you cannot put the full percentages in the savings accounts this week, put in what you can, but don't fail to set money aside in savings because you feel you don't have enough. Just do it, little bits every week, and you will soon find that you have a snowball effect going on with buckets of cash filling up and bills still getting paid.

Staying Sane and Staying Safe

You will find that once you start using this system of managing your cash flow, you will come to rely on it and you will sleep better at night knowing that you are in control of the money. The great news is that, since this is a planning tool, you can start using the system right now, today. No waiting is required for just the right time.

Finding out what your income planning target really needs to be will increase your demand for income and that demand needs to be placed on everyone in the company to make more income and not waste one dime on foolish things that don't produce more income or dramatically increase efficiencies.

After you use this system for a while you will be like thousands of my clients who wonder how they ever survived without this system and say things like, "If I had known about and used this system 10 years ago I'd be a millionaire by now."

I want to share another testimonial, and this one is from Dr. G, a cosmetic dentist who only treats celebrities and professional athletes. I was giving a seminar a few years ago, and I saw Dr. G in the audience and I knew he had started using my software system. So at the end of the seminar I found him and asked him to tell me his story and here is what he said:

Testimonial

"I make $200,000 a month and I spend $200,000 a month. I'm 63 years old and have no retirement savings because I wasted most of my money. This system is putting the discipline in place for me to finally put my exit plan into action and retire without having to worry about money." - Dr. G.

So you see, even the so-called rich people can be unhappy with their financial condition. They get over extended buying houses, cars, boats, traveling, etc. and their spouses are big spenders too, so they have a lot of everything…EXCEPT financial security.

How to Think and Plan in Futures

A critical element in the Cash Flow Mojo system is how to allocate cash for paying bills. When it comes to paying bills, there are a few tips that can help you weather the stress of starting to use the system when your income is not yet where it needs to be to make your income planning target.

One action that can take stress off is to allocate a bit of cash each week for large bills that are difficult to pay. For example if you find it difficult to pay the mortgage or rent on your building then allocate 25% of the payment from each week's income and set that aside so when the time comes to pay the bill you only have to come up with the final 25% instead of scrambling to come up with 100% in one week.

I even use this strategy with insurance payments that I pay once a year, like auto insurance. I divide the premium by 52 weeks and I set aside that small amount every week in a separate bank account so when I get the bill for the annual premium I have the cash sitting there to pay it in full.

The same thing applies to large purchases like a new piece of equipment or a new delivery van for the company. Figure out how when you want to buy the equipment or the van. Then divide the anticipated cost by the number of weeks until then and set that much aside every week until you have the cash to pay for the item without financing. And then, of course since Cash Is King, be sure to negotiate a big discount for paying cash.

That's how cash flow management planning is done BEFORE the money comes in and BEFORE it is spent.

Mistake

(Flying by the seat of your pants) – Deciding to buy on credit with no idea how you are going to pay.

Solution

(Thinking and Planning in futures) – Deciding to buy something, and saving up the cash for it. Buy it using a credit card, then immediately paying off the credit card purchase with the saved up cash.

Now let's quickly look at the last two steps of the sequence. That's step 4, where you approve the plan and get whoever is going to do the cash transfers to savings accounts or pay the bills to carry out exactly what is approved, and then finally step 5 which is recording that in your accounting system.

Then you immediately start the cycle over again for the new week that you are already in by doing income planning in step number 1.

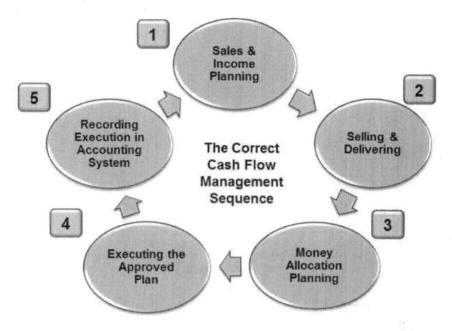

I have a caution to give you here. This cash flow management system has proven itself to work, time and time again. But, as we talked about at the beginning of this book, it is a different way of operating from standard accounting. So you may run into some resistance from people who cannot think with this system, and will try to revert you back to the old way of using your money – the way they are comfortable with – or even tell you that you don't need to use this system, or that it takes too long.

Don't be fooled. This entire cycle can be done in 20 to 30 minutes a week using the software tool we have developed to implement this system.

Plus, using the old accounting methods got you where you are today, and if you want to substantially improve your financial condition, then you need to make some changes.

Albert Einstein defined insanity as doing the same thing over and over again and expecting a different result.

So this system grooves in different habits on how you handle money so you can get the result you are looking for.

Testimonial

"Two years ago my construction company was close to bankruptcy with about $30 in our bank account and no way to pay bills. Using this Cash Flow Management program we are doing so well now. With the power of this system and the financial stability it has helped us create, we now have plenty of cash in reserves and always have more operating capital than we need in our bank operating account." - K. A.

The One Word That Can Make You Wealthy

I'll share a secret about what my clients have learned that helps them get out of debt and get very wealth very fast while using this system. They learn to say "NO" when it comes to spending money.

I have taken on clients for private coaching that were only days away from filing bankruptcy and I make them agree to my rules to take them on as a private coaching client. The first rule is that they cannot spend any money without my okay and if they do I fire them and will not work with them any longer. Then I put them on the Cash Flow Mojo® software system and when they ask to spend money on something that will not get them closer to solvency I say NO.

They call me the "NO Witch" because I say NO most of the time, but I get a good result when it comes to getting the company out of debt and getting the business owner on the road to financial solvency and wealth building. At first the client may moan and groan, but it doesn't take long before they see progress being made and financial improvement happening, and then they are smiling and sleeping really well at night.

So learn to say NO when it comes to spending money outside the Cash Flow Mojo system, or spending on things that do not improve the income or efficiencies of the business. When it comes to spending money, learning to use that one little word at the right times can make you a millionaire.

Thanks Dr. P! That's my reward for doing what I do. There is no better feeling in the world than knowing I have helped yet another business owner take charge of their financial future, get in front of the 8-ball, and get firmly on the road to solvency and wealth.

Raise My Prices (Gasp!) In THIS ECONOMY?

It's a tough economy out there and (Gasp!) the cost of doing business is rising about 8 – 12% a year.

What? You say...Why, the government said the cost of living has only gone up 3%.

Yes, the government says that every year because they have to give Social Security recipients a COLA (Cost Of Living Adjustment) raise every year based on the percentage they announce. So of course they aren't going to be honest about the percentage. The price of groceries alone has gone up 30% in the past six months. The government is forcing our seniors into poverty with an annual COLA of only 3%.

Business owners are in the same boat. Your suppliers raise prices or add a line item for a hefty fuel charge on deliveries hoping you don't notice, and you need to pass those increases on to your customers or they will eat away at your profits until you are insolvent.

Cash Flow Mojo® Tip #8

Religiously monitor increases in costs and make adjustments to maximize profits.

You must raise your prices to keep up with the cost of doing business, but figuring out how to raise prices without offending or alarming your customers is crucial.

I'll give you an example of a smart way to raise prices, and that is my favorite coffee company, Starbucks. They raise their prices in very tiny increments a few times a year. One day my cup of black coffee is $1.41 with tax and the next week it is $1.46 with tax. Yes I notice, but I immediately justify it by saying to myself, well it's only a nickel and I do love the coffee so I'll pay the increase. Then four months later my cup of coffee is $1.51 with tax, and again I say, well... it's only a nickel...

That's brilliant! Instead of raising an item a huge amount all at once, raise it in small increments several times a year.

I've been going to the same dentist for years and every year the cost of getting my teeth cleaned goes up $10. I'm used to it. I expect it. And more importantly, I justify it for them because I am a business owner and I know that rent, payroll, utilities, lab fees and dental supplies go up every year.

Consumers are not stupid. They know your costs go up. They expect a raise from their employer every year so they know their employer's costs go up. So when you never raise prices they start thinking you must be desperate for business because your competitors are all charging more.

If you do have to make it a substantial increase, do something for the customer to ease the shock. You can give current customers a chance to buy at the old price for a few days before the increase so if they don't take you up on that offer then they are the ones who are saying they are willing to pay the new price later. Or bundle it with another item to raise the perceived value of the item at a new "bundle" price. Or give some extra service that costs you nothing along with the higher priced item for a limited time.

The fact is you have to keep raising your prices to keep up with increasing costs of inventory, supplies, and raw materials to maintain your profitability after cost of goods. And to keep up with the rise in overhead expenses as well. Raising the number of unit sales on a decreasingly profitable product will have you headed for bankruptcy in no time. Ignore this at your peril.

What Money Is

Money is a commodity that can be likened to being the fuel in the gas tank of life. Everyone needs a consistently full tank to operate successfully and achieve their financial goals.

Now, you know when you are driving down the road and your gas tank needle is hovering on empty, you can't enjoy the passing scenery, you can't have a decent conversation with the person in the passenger seat next to you, and you can't even enjoy singing along to the song on the radio. Your attention is laser focused on where to find the next gas station to fill up the tank.

But when the tank is full your attention can be on enjoying the ride through life.

I don't want you running through your business life on empty because you start looking in desperation at your customers as wallets instead of people to be attended to with high quality products and great customer service.

That's why I developed the Cash Flow Mojo® software system. So you can learn to use this system yourself without any hand-holding from me unless you really need help to get through some super-serious situation. If you need that, I can do it through one-on-one private coaching. I've turned many a company around, dug them out of debt, and even pulled them back from the brink of bankruptcy.

If you learn this cash flow management system, and live this system in your business and even your personal life, you will be the master of your own financial destiny. That helps you, it helps your employees, your family, your neighbors, your town and state and it helps all of us because you are helping the economy of those areas to improve.

The Deadly Trio

There is a simple reason why you can work your rear end off to get ahead financially but get stonewalled and suffer unexpected setbacks along the way and end up being unhappy with your financial condition. I call it the Deadly Trio.

First, in your entire education, the curriculum didn't include teaching you the correct way to manage your money to *your own best advantage*, so I know you didn't just sleep through the class.

Second, you haven't had the proper tools to help you *take charge of* and *stay in control of* your finances. That's sort of like trying to drive a nail in a board without a hammer.

And lastly, and most deadly, there are others out there who want to control *your* money for *their own financial advantage*: the two worst offenders are the credit card companies who do everything they can to keep you on the payments-for-life-plan, and the government which uses the tax system to control you into giving them more and more of your hard-earned money.

So you can see that taking charge of your finances isn't rocket science, or complicated, or mysterious. It requires 3 simple things:

1 - Having the right tools,

2 – The willingness to learn to use the tools properly, and

3 - The self-discipline to stay on the right path and moving toward YOUR personal financial goals.

If you saw the movie *The Matrix* you might remember when Neo said to Morpheus "There's a difference between knowing the path and walking the path." And that's absolutely true with this cash flow management system. You have to walk the path to arrive at your goals.

Now, here's a shameless plug for my software system:

Fortunately, you can do this whole cash flow planning action yourself very quickly and very simply in about 20 minutes a week using the Cash Flow Mojo® software.

There is video training on every aspect of the software system built right in, and group coaching sessions you can attend to get your questions answered.

You can get a 30-day trial for less than the price of lunch. Try it out and then participate in the monthly subscription plan for as long as you need or want to use the software. There are no long-term contracts to buy, and you and your financial team can access the software on the Internet from any computer anywhere you happen to be in the world where you have an Internet connection.

To learn more about the cash flow management system, just go to www.CashflowMojoSoftware.com and take advantage of the 30-day trial offer.

Promote It Right and They WILL Come

Advertising and promotion is a science and an art. It takes creative copywriting, attention grabbing graphics, effective eye trails the viewer can follow and effective offers and calls-to-action to get the potential customer to do what you want them to do - BUY your stuff.

Long before the art part begins though, there is the careful crafting of a product or service offer that will not only be attractive to the consumer, but will result in both adequate sales and PROFITS after all costs including advertising costs, labor and sales commissions.

Deciding what to promote and how to promote it can be simplified by doing a few steps BEFORE that all important weekly sales and income planning meeting. That way you can easily decide what offer you'll be promoting to support your sales team and how much funding you'll need depending on how you'll be promoting it: TV and radio are a lot more expensive than direct mail or Internet marketing.

I've done this with my clients many times and they have boomed their sales because of doing these few simple actions, so let's get started.

Step 1 - Make a list of all of the products and services you have to sell. Now if you are in a retail store business this can be groupings of products or individual products. Keeping it simple is best.

Step 2 - Rank each individual product or service from 1 to 5 (1 being the highest and 5 being the lowest) in these 3 categories:

Customer Demand

Profitability

Ease of Delivery

Whatever products or services you have that are ranked highest across all the categories are the products that you should be promoting with your advertising budget.

Keep in mind, promoting doesn't necessarily mean discounting the product or service itself. In fact I would prefer you not discount your products and services because the customer starts to devalue them. You can add little extras that don't cost you much of anything that would be highly desirable to the consumer. If you are promoting furnace servicing to get ready for winter you might offer a no-obligation complete HVAC checkup, and a service warranty on your work, or extended evening hours without an overtime charge for the convenience of working people.

List all of the products and services you currently sell and the retail price of each.	Rank 1 - 5 (1 = Highest and 5 = Lowest)			
Rank each one on a scale of 1 to 5 for each attribute	Retail $	Customer Demand	Profitability	Ease of Delivery

A construction client's high demand, high profit item was building decks onto houses. One of the most successful promotions they did was make a "Cleanup Promise Guarantee" that they would completely clean up the site, including using a magnet to pick up all loose nails and screws that may have fallen into the grass so the customer's barefoot kids wouldn't step on a sharp nail and hurt themselves. Their sales went through the roof because they became known around town as the company with the Cleanup Promise Guarantee.

If you have a product or service that is highly profitable but not much in demand, then you might figure out a way to bundle that with something that is in high demand and profitable. Product or service bundling can be very effective at increasing the sale and having something attractive to promote.

Add-ons are like bundling but are more of an upsell type of offer. One of the most innovative ones I've come across lately was a store that sells batteries. I bought a watch battery for $4.95 and was told that for an additional $8.95 I could get free watch battery replacements for life on that specific watch only. Well that was a no brainer for me because I've had my watch for 14 years and love it enough that I've replaced the band two times and the battery every two years, so I spent the $8.95 without question. I got a card describing my watch to bring in for the free batteries for life. They tripled their sale and are counting on the fact that most people won't keep their watch for more than 2 more battery changes, or they will lose their card that they have to bring in to get the free battery. Smart upselling!

New services that you create can be winners as well. A friend of mine who is a fellow accountant took my lead and started offering a tax planning strategy session to his clients during the summer and again in November for a pre-paid annual fee so they would have plenty of time to make any financial moves necessary to reduce their upcoming tax liability. In what are traditionally slow months he filled his calendar and raised his income substantially; and his clients loved the service.

Carpet cleaning companies all across the nation have added tile and grout cleaning to their stable of services. Dentists have added teeth whitening, and car wash companies have added on-site detailing or "We Come to You" services where they pick up your car and deliver it back to your home or office after it is cleaned.

So, the science is what to promote that will get the most sales for the most profit after all expenses.

The art is how to promote it - what media vehicle(s) you will use and what you will say with the copy and the graphics.

I would be remiss if I didn't mention Internet marketing and encourage you to utilize the amazing power of the Internet to get your message out to your target audience, whether you are doing public relations, branding messages, or advertising and promoting.

I was talking with Brian Dawson, CEO at Customer Finder® Marketing, our subsidiary company www.CustomerFinderMarketing.com and he was giving me the statistics on Internet marketing.

A huge majority (over 80%) of consumers, age 35 to 65, are making their buying decisions by looking on the Internet for suppliers of what they want to buy from dentures to diamonds. They rely on the search engines to dish up vendors in their town for exactly what they type into the search bar. They look at websites, read blog articles, watch Internet video ads, and ask their friends on

Facebook, and Twitter and their colleagues on LinkedIn for recommendations.

After Google, the number two search engine is YouTube. An unbelievable 28+ billion videos are watched every week on YouTube in the United States alone, and many of those videos are short advertising commercials that link right back to the company's website.

Because an Internet article or video ad stays on the Internet until you take it down, it is like a sales person working 24/7 for you all year long. That means you have a much better chance of getting a long term return on your advertising dollars spent than for offline marketing that gets stuck in a drawer or thrown in the trash like a postcard, or plays on TV while your potential customer is in the kitchen getting a snack.

Now I'm not denigrating offline marketing at all. It can be very effective and can really help your sales. There are some who still rely on the newspaper, direct mail and the yellow pages phone book to find what they need. I'm just pointing out that the new wave of shopping is being done on the Internet on computers and cell phones, so you need to be there too. I guarantee you your competition is there.

It's never too late to get started using the Internet to promote your business and there are many fast, cost effective ways to do Internet marketing. You just need to use reputable companies that really know what they are doing and can deliver measurable results.

If you need some help getting started with or improving the sales conversions of your website or Internet video or pay-per-click ads, or have questions about your Internet marketing plan, contact Brian at Customer Finder® Marketing. www.CustomerFinderMarketing.com

Part of the science is figuring out what a new customer is worth to you over the period of a year or the lifetime of a customer, and then figure out how much you would be willing to spend to get a new customer. For example the value of a new patient for a regular or cosmetic dentist might be $8,000 to $100,000 over the lifetime of the patient. Spending a few thousand to get one new patient is reasonable. But, for a carpet cleaning company the value of a new customer may be $2,000 over a lifetime so spending a few hundred to get a new customer would make more sense to that company.

Coming up with a reasonable monthly advertising budget to get the number of new patients or customers you need to maintain growth and solvency is crucial. Spending the money on the most effective and cost efficient media vehicles is equally as important, and measuring the return on your advertising investment is vital.

When you find something that works well, stick with it until it no longer works. If you try something new, give it a fair chance to work and if it doesn't deliver, drop it or modify it and move onto something different. It may be the offer that is not pulling rather than the vehicle itself that isn't working for you.

Cash Flow Mojo® Tip #9

Always measure the return on investment of
sales activities and promotional spending.

My Story

Some of you may be wondering about how I have done handling money. In fact, two of the questions many business owners ask me is, "Did you ever go broke?" and "How did you pull out of bad financial situations?"

So here's the real story…the booms and busts…and the busts were really big. I'll tell you about those and also share what I learned from each one.

In the mid-1970s in Virginia I started a marketing business with two partners, and we did really well. In 1982 I decided to sell my share of the business to my partners and move to Texas for personal reasons.

The fatal mistake I made was making a verbal agreement that my partners could pay me over time for my share of the company. I financed their purchase, and ended up not getting paid one dime. I was living almost 2,000 miles away, and had zero money for a legal battle so I lost it all. That was the first financial bust.

I learned two lessons from that:

Lesson # 1- I'm not a bank and I shouldn't try to act like a bank by lending other people money.

Lesson # 1

If you're not a bank, don't try to act like a bank.
Don't lend other people money.

Lesson # 2 - Money agreements, while they are being formed and are all roses and light, should be in the form of an ironclad written agreement that will stand up in court.

I've seen a lot of "agreements" go sour and that can create a real financial mess, and the one I made was no exception.

Lesson # 2

All agreements should be in written form that will stand up in court, especially agreements that concern business deals or money.

I had to borrow money for rent and groceries until I landed an account executive job with Kenyon and Eckhardt Advertising Agency in Houston working on the McDonald's account.

For the next 15 years I was working for major advertising agencies and on the corporate side of business in companies owned by Pepsico and The Southland Corporation being a marketing executive and buyer. I was pulling in really good money and recovered financially.

Early on in my career, I had decided that I wanted to be wealthy. So I learned from working in many businesses, watching how they handled money, and by reading every book I could find on business finance.

Each book had one or two golden nuggets of information that were pieces of the puzzle about how to handle money in business correctly.

In the mid-1980s I was hired by The Southland Corporation 7-Eleven Stores headquarters in Dallas, Texas in an advertising management position and then as a Regional Buyer. I worked there over nine years and during that time I watched this company pull in multi-millions of dollars and yet slowly go broke despite massive layoffs every year and severe cost cutting measures, until finally they filed bankruptcy and were bought out by one of their foreign franchisees who knew how to manage cash flow correctly.

I learned a lot from the new owners of the corporation about cash flow management. I tested the principles I learned by applying them to my own personal income, and they worked like magic.

In 1995 I left Southland, opened my own company, and started doing accounting and teaching this cash flow management system to business owners in Dallas.

Then I made another fatal mistake. I was married to a man who owned his own business and was making bad mistakes with money that I was not made aware of.

In fact I wasn't paying attention either, so there was responsibility on both sides. I just assumed he would be fiscally responsible in his business. Bad mistake to not ask questions and ask for financial reports to observe what was really happening

 In 1996 I got the news flash that the IRS was after him for over $200,000 and that we were personally liable for that amount because it involved payroll taxes. Even worse, the IRS wanted the money within 30 days.

We sold our house for what little equity we had in it, auctioned off everything of high value in the house and moved into an apartment. We fired all the staff in the engineering company, sold all the equipment, and my husband did all the work at home and we used all that income to help pay the IRS.

I worked like mad using this cash flow management formula to pull us out and pay off that debt. The miraculous thing was, using the formula in this book, that debt to the IRS was paid off in only 14 months.

The lesson I learned that time was:

Lesson # 3 - You need to know what is happening with your money, whether it's your personal money or the money in a business your immediate family owns or that you are a partner in. What you don't know *can* hurt you.

Lesson # 3

When it comes to money, ignorance is NOT bliss.
What you don't know CAN hurt you.

I moved away to Florida and started again to re-build financially.

What pulled me through each of those catastrophes was using this cash flow management formula myself. It's not complicated or mysterious. It is a simple formula based on generally accepted accounting principles that have been in use for thousands of years, combined with common sense actions in managing money.

At the same time I was recovering financially, I was still coaching other business owners from written notes and checklists on using the formula. I knew instinctively that my income would be capped by how many business owners I could reach out to and help. I decided that I needed to create a software program that business owners could use to do this cash flow management planning system themselves, unless they really needed one-one-one coaching.

Until I did it, I knew nothing about developing software. I just had a burning passion for sharing this system to help business owners get and stay solvent despite what the general economy was doing.

What a great experience to have worked with so many business owners to test my products and services. To pull them out of the soup, get them out of debt, pull them back from the brink of bankruptcy and help them get their feet onto the road of financial freedom, where they expected their business to take them in the first place.

My first software product was launched in 2006 and is in use in 25 countries around the world in companies in over 50 different industries.

My new software product **Cash Flow Mojo**® is even more powerful and can help even more business owners because it is an on-line application that can be accessed by anyone anywhere with an Internet connection and a computer device that links to the Internet. How cool is that?

Further Education

My company, Money Management Solutions, Inc., is a business that is dedicated to improving the financial condition of businesses and their owners.

Books, Courses, Software

Through the parent company there are books, training materials and the Cash Flow Mojo® online software program available for your education and use.

www.CashFlowMojoSoftware.com

Private Coaching

Subscribers to the online Cash Flow Mojo® software have access to group coaching as a complimentary part of that service.

Some businesses owners in certain financial situations desire fast, personalized, private coaching on a one-on-one basis. There are a number of coaching modules available that cover:

1 – Financial Review and Recommendations

2 – Customized solutions

3 – Implementation of Customized Solutions and Cash Flow Mojo® management and planning cycles

4 – Monitoring

5 – Results Review

The business must be subscribed to and using the Cash Flow Mojo® software program to qualify for one-on-one private coaching.

Seminars and Webinars

From time to time, I will speak at seminars or give online webinars. Unless the events are for private companies or groups, they will be announced in mailings to my customers who have purchased products through my website(s). You can also get advance notice of these events by signing up on my website for the tips and newsletters that go out to the interested public.

www.CashFlowMojoSoftware.com

A Challenge and a Promise

My challenge to you is to use this cash flow management system every week for a minimum of 6 months exactly as it is presented and is intended to be used: no shortcuts, no leaving out steps or changing steps, no spending money on anything except what it is allocated for and no over spending your weekly income. Above all, you must participate in the management process every week; no whining and no quitting.

If you do this, I promise you that your business will be in a better financial condition, that you will be in control of your financial future, and that you will have cash savings in the bank and be sleeping much better at night than when you started.

You will have Cash Flow Mojo!

You'll wonder how you ever survived without it.

Glossary

Accounting – A financial record keeping system that records how much money came into a company or household, and what that money was spent on. It is basically a report of what happened in the past with the money. It is necessary for preparing reports for tax filing purposes.

Balance Sheet – An itemized report showing the assets owned by a company, liabilities owed by a company and the equity of a company as of a certain date.

Buckets of Cash – A term coined by Sandra Simmons that refers to bank savings accounts that have a specific purpose in the Cash Flow Mojo® software system for the funds placed in them; purposes such as protecting the company, increasing the net worth of the company, expanding the company and long-term wealth building for the owners of the company.

Budget – A Calculation of the amount of income needed each week to not only run the company, but to do better than break even and achieve the company's financial goals; planning on how to get in the needed amount of income; then allocating the actual income to achieve those goals without overspending the income. The budget becomes the sales and income planning target.

Cash Flow – The money flowing into a company from sales and flowing back out of a company for cost of goods sold, expenses, investments, assets and liabilities.

Cash Flow Management – The actions taken to plan and control the amount of money coming into a company and the amount and use of money flowing out of a company as expenditures, investments or savings.

Cash Flow Mojo – 1. Seemingly magical powers to bring about increases in the income of a company and to use that cash in a manner that keeps the company financially stable and able to achieve the financial goals of the company. 2. The trademarked name of a software system that helps business owners correctly manage their cash flow to their own financial advantage.

Cost of Goods Sold – How much is paid for goods, materials or services to produce a product that is then sold.

Credit Card Debt (Revolving Credit Debt) – The amount owed on standard revolving credit card debt such as purchases made with credit cards.

Discretionary Expenses – Expense items that are desired rather than being necessary to sustain the operation and increase its production.

Economy - The production and consumption of goods and services of a community regarded as a whole; a business or a household are each an economy that are part of the larger economies of their city, state and country.

Flourish – 1. To do well and be prosperous. 2. To be in a state of activity and production. 3. To reach a height of development or influence. 4. To increase in health, wealth, happiness, honor, comfort or whatever is desirable.

Forecast - To predict (a future condition or happening)

Income Planning (Sales and Income Planning) – The purpose of the sales and income planning activity is to insure that specific plans are in place to reach the income planning target in the current week. This planning consists of setting targets and quotas for each employee responsible for making sales, and collecting accounts receivable. It also includes planning the promotional activities within the weekly promotion budget to insure that and adequate return on investment is achieved in the form of new sales income.

Income Planning Target – 1. The amount of income needed weekly to do much better than just being able to pay the bills. 2. The amount of sales income needed weekly to do much better than break-even.

Mojo – Magical powers

Money Management – (also cash flow management) The actions taken to affect and control the amount of money coming into a company and the amount and use of money flowing out of a company or held by a company.

Operating Basis – The principles and policies on which a company operates overall or in a specific area such as finances.

Planning – The action of figuring out a way to do something in advance.

Profit & Loss Report (P&L) – An itemized report of the income and expenses of a company which shows the net income after expenses over a certain period of time.

Revolving Debt - This type of debt typically has a variable interest rate, an open-ended term and payments that are based on a percentage of the balance; credit card debt is revolving debt.

Sales and Income Planning (Income Planning) – The purpose of the sales and income planning activity is to insure that plans are in place to reach the income planning target in the current week. This planning consists of setting targets and quotas for each employee responsible for making sales, and collecting accounts receivable. It also includes planning the promotional activities within the weekly promotion budget to insure that and adequate return on investment is achieved in the form of new sales income.

Solvency – 1. The state of a company being able to service its debt and meet its other obligations, especially in the long-term. 2. The state of a company having more cash and assets than liabilities.

Viable – Able to survive

Viewpoint - 1. A mental position from which things are viewed. 2. A position from which something is observed or considered.

Made in the USA
Lexington, KY
10 March 2018